90 Years of Memories
by
Pauline Mary & Geoffrey Walker

1930 to 2020

Geoffrey Walker born
September 28th, 1930,
The Hermitage farm,
(now a private dwelling)
Strawberry Lane.
Whitwick, Leicestershire.

Pauline Marry Ward born
November 29th, 1933
9 Station Road Bagworth,
(now demolished)
Leicestershire.

We are grateful to our New Zealand friend

Lesley Baker

For her advice on a

voice to text manuscript.

Also, the brilliant book cover

By

Nicole Lewis

During these last few years, I've been gradually losing my central vision due to macular deterioration, although I can see to get about without any problem.

However. if I focus on a person's face or the keyboard that part disappears.
All is not lost and I now use voice to text and read back.
Member of Blind veterans UK

We do hope that you enjoy a brief glimpse into our family life.
Love and best wishes Pauline and Geoffrey

Chapter 1
Geoffrey, The first 7 Years

My first ever memory was being taken for a walk along Strawberry Lane in my pram.
I can clearly remember the very spot to this day and have visited it many times.
High stone walls thickly covered in dark green ivy lined that part of the lane.

Grandma and Grandpa Walker were the farm tenants.
Life was good, playing around with the chickens collecting their eggs and listening to the large red cockerel proclaiming his territory.
Paddy the dog was my constant companion.
A small stream meandered its way through the orchard, disappearing underground as it passed the front of the farmhouse, finally discharged into the nearby reservoir.
The only other child I remember seeing was my cousin Jean.
They came to stay for a week's holiday every summer. Traveling by bus from Swanwick in Derbyshire.
We have always remained the best of friends.

I don't remember who took me to the Oaks in Charnwood school on the first day but it was probably my mother. We walked the 1 ½ miles along the country farm road, passing Drybrook farm (later to become my second home) past One Barrow Lodge farm (now demolished) and so to school.

Mrs. Thompson was the only teacher of five to nine-year-old children. A very poor school photograph shows 16 children with Mrs. Thompson I am right-hand side sucking my thumb.

I spent over two very unhappy years at that school.

Billy Heritage was the school bully.

He often promised lie in wait for me along the woodland lane and hang me from a tree.

Mildred Bowley caused bedlam one day as she got one of the counters stuck up her nose, I liked Mildred I remember that she had long ginger plaits.

Other memories of my two years at The Oaks

Nativity play in the church hall. My small garden blooming with cornflowers. Lessons on the blackboard, pupils used slate and chalk and at the end of the day, we wiped our slate clean.

After being taken to school and collected for the first few days I then had to make my way there and back, sometimes they were very scary.

Once as I was walking along the forest pathway a fox ran right in front of me, scared me stiff.

During the summer evenings, I remember mum taking me for walks were met up with this strange man.

No explanation was ever given to me who he was, and I don't remember ever asking.

He was always very kind and occasionally we went back to his house in the village.

I had visited this house in the village of Whitwick quite a few times with my mother in the past.

The flush toilet had always fascinated me because on the farm and at school we only had earth toilets.

However, this time it was obvious we were staying as my bed was made upon the landing, with only two rooms in the cottage, one taken by an old lady. Mother had got married that wary day and occupied the other bedroom.

The cottage (now demolished) consisted of a living kitchen with a stone sink and a cold-water tap fastened over on a block of wood.

The coal-fired black leaded fire grate had a water boiler one side and an oven the other.

A pine scrubbed top table `and chairs were the only other furniture. A small pantry was under the staircase. The front room consisted of a large portrait of a World War One soldier, and a glass jar on the windowsill with a stickleback fish swimming around. I am sure it would have had other furniture. The old lady became known as grandma Griffin and was always saying crazy things and very scary. I have since realized that she was suffering from dementia.

Chapter 2
Pauline Starts School 1938

Pauline's first memory is of her starting infants' school in September of 1938. I was a coal mining village (now residential) in south Leicestershire.

Long rows of terraced housing belonging to the mining company flanked each side of the main road. The mine headstocks belching volumes of steam and black smoke stood next to Pauline's parents' house. Starting school was not a trauma for Pauline, at least half a dozen of her friends started at the same time.

Pauline clearly remembers people shouting out, "we are at war." September 3rd, 1939.

The night of the German Luftwaffe bombing Coventry although 30 miles distant brightly illuminated the night sky with the burning of the city.

This news item is taken from the web.

The Coventry blitz was a series of bombing raids that took place in the English city of Coventry. The city was bombed many times during the Second World War by the German Air Force. The most devastating of these attacks occurred on the evening of 14 November 1940 and continued into the morning of 15 November

Chapter 3
Geoffrey, July 1938/45

My arrival in the last class of Whitwick infants' school just a few weeks before the August holidays left me in shock.
At least 20 boys and girls all my age, I had never been so scared.
One thing I will remember seeing is a large Rocking horse stored in the corner of the classroom.
If you were very good you were allowed to ride on this beautiful horse.
I never did get to try it out but in my later years, I made one for our family.
One day as I returned home from school I was greeted with the cry of a baby, brother William (always known as Bill) had arrived.

Shortly after we moved to a house in a row of two-bedroom cottages.
Grandmother Griffin stayed on at the cottage, unfortunately, I have no memory of her eventual death or funeral.
Freddie Burton was our landlord, he also owned a similar row of cottages in the village that still exist on Dumps road.
I remember he lived in a splendid house and rode his horse to hound.

I vividly remember Grandpa Walker talking about an impending conflict with Germany. One day I watched a flight of Tiger Moth biplanes practicing low-level flight in formation over the reservoir. I have since learned that they belonged to the 'Elementary Flying School' stationed at Desford.

To hear one aircraft, we all rushed outside but as I recall three or four at eye level was amazing.

This became a regular feature over the coming years; however, this was building up to a tragedy waiting to happen. I will explain later

My first wartime memory was a line of children walking up the street with brown nametags pinned to their lapel, and a box containing a gas mask slung over their shoulder. They were schoolchildren of all ages, evacuated from Birmingham.

Some had billets already agreed; unfortunately, some were without a place to stay.

That is how we came to have a boy of about my age to stay with us, in an overcrowded two-bed cottage, with a shared outside WC.

A bed was made up for him on the floor against mine, however, he soon became unwell, he then had my bed and I had a turn on the floor.

As far as I remember he stayed less than a week before his parents came to take him back home.

The largest contingent of evacuees came from the English Martyrs School in Birmingham. All attended Whitwick Holy Cross school.

Whitwick Historical Group have an excellent booklet entitled 'Whitwick Schools at War

Opposite our row of cottages on Talbot Street, and next to the 'Prince of Wales' public house (now unoccupied) stood, and still stands today, a green space which contained two concrete Underground air-raid shelters.

As I remember these contained a row of slatted seating down each side and a row down the center.

Water lay on the floor through a lack of drainage giving off a most unpleasant smell.

Although the air raid sirens went many times I only remember spending one night in the shelters.

Most people constructed Anderson type shelters in their gardens equipping them with what comforts they could. All the cottages in the row were two up and two down with a built-on scullery containing a shallow sink, cold-water tap, and a coal-fired copper with a wooden lid.

Monday was wash day in every home, many competing for the brightest wash.

Friday was bath night, cleanest first.

That was the type of accommodation most working-class families lived in up until the mid-1940s.

Now there was another very important establishment in the vicinity; Russel's Fish and Chip shop.

Fish were rarely on the menu, but we did have battered rice cakes along with chips; us kids were always looking to have a pennyworth of scratchings with our Friday penny.

The coal-fired frying range was able to be seen at the Snibston Discovery Park museum until its recent closure.

I loved standing there thinking of times past.

In 1941 I took the 11+ exam. It was recorded that there were 248 village children, plus 18 evacuees at the Whitwick C of E school.

I didn't pass for Grammar School, but to Broomleys secondary modern school; those who failed stayed on until they were

14 years of age. Starting work mostly in the coal mines or the brickyards.

Most boys from the age of 11 had Saturday jobs, as labor was in short supply.
I helped on my uncle's farm that was situated opposite the Monastery of Mount St. Bernard.
Nearby was an RAF listening station known as the "beam benders." This was used to transmit false radio signals to passing squadrons of enemy bombers flying on a transmitted radio beam to their target.

My uncle eventually bought me a second-hand bicycle, so I didn't have to walk to and from the farm. It was nearby that major wartime incidents took place,
Around 1942 saw the farm lanes turned into roadside ammunition dumps.
Anderson shelters were spaced out at regular intervals and filled with grenades, 303 ammunition, etc.
These were attractive places for schoolchildren, and more than one boy suffered permanent damage through the explosion.

February of that year saw Whitwick's first major air disaster, it was a Vickers Wellington bomber flown by Sergeant J

Andrew RAFVR age 20. Plus, a crew of four.

I visited the crash site on my uncle's farm the next day, it was completely burnt out. It had crashed against a line of trees at the edge of a 20-acre field.

The crash is logged as: -

The aircraft had taken off at 1130hrs from Castle Donington on a cross-country navigational exercise. At some point the aircraft flew through a snowstorm, resulting in severe icing. The aircraft lost height and stalled whilst trying to pull up over a pinnacle of rock, crashing at 1630 hrs. near Gun Hill Whitwick. Sadly, all the crew was killed.

That was the first time the full meaning of war came home to me, previously I thought of it as a great adventure. I couldn't wait to be old enough to join the RAF as a pilot.

At one-point people with shotguns were issued with cartridges loaded with a steel ball instead of lead shot.

Instructions were given on how to take aim at invading paratroopers.

I never saw one even fired in practice; for fear of the shotgun exploding.

The 2nd July that year saw the Tiger Moth crash into Blackbrook reservoir.

Several aircraft were doing low-level flying
as I described previously,
when the undercarriage of one aircraft
touched the surface of the water.
It was immediately brought down and sank.
The other planes in the flight landed
nearby, the pilots along with an uncle of
mine attempting a rescue.
Using a rowing boat, they searched in vain
for the pilot.
The next day I watched as Flight Sergeant
J E Ratigan RCAF was recovered.
He was laid to rest in the Ibstock cemetery.
LE67 6LG
After that flying didn't seem quite so
attractive.

Chapter 4
Dig for Victory

Most schools had vegetable plots under the national slogan 'Dig for Victory' at Broomleys school it was called the 'Food Plot'.
I am unsure if girls helped in this work.
School meals were very good; my favorite was cheese and potato pie.
Can't remember what we had for pudding, but we did have one probably with custard.

When I was 13 years old I gained a place at Loughborough College, another shock to the system, an all-boys school of some 500 pupils. During the August holiday, I went to harvest camp at Hose organized by the college.
Local schoolchildren went potato picking, and general harvesting organized by local schools.
No such thing as health and safety.
Towards the end of 1944, a German soldier was dropped off each day to work on uncle's farm. His name was Otto Schrader.
Otto was taken prisoner in the western desert, one of Rommel's men.
We exchanged language lessons as we went about our work, it was six months

after the war ended that he was repatriated home, to his wife and two boys.

Finally, I recount some of the day-to-day memories of my schoolboy days during that period.

Like the blackout, it must be difficult for youngsters nowadays to imagine a total black night, food rationing, with no such word as child obesity.

The distinctive drone of enemy aircraft overhead, even a bomb dropped on Thringstone. Searchlights trying to pick out enemy aircraft, and the flashes in the sky as Anti-Aircraft gunners tried to find their target.

During one week of school holiday, I was a telegram boy at Coalville PO.

One delivery was to Barden; it contained a message that a relative had been killed in action, not the best of days.

We played cricket and football.

Games with the girls were shinty, tin-a-lerky, and rounders, not to mention hide and seek.

On Monday evening, 5 June 1944 we watched as the sky filled with Dakota aircraft towing Horsa gliders.
We realized something big was about to happen; it was of cause the D Day landings.

I continued helping my uncle on the form at every opportunity earning a little pocket money until I finally left school in August of 1945.

Dad was a coal miner not only during the war but throughout is working life. He suffered from terrible accidents in the mine and one time got caught in an underground fire.
After brother Bill came Evelyn, Fred, Marjorie, and Richard.
Fred as a young boy became a victim of poliomyelitis and wore a caliper on one leg for the rest of his life.

After the war mum and dad bought a new build, a semidetached house with flush toilet downstairs, and one upstairs also in a proper bathroom. They remained in the same house until the end of their lives.

Chapter 5
Pauline in the 1940s

Pauline's family moved to a different house belonging to the colliery.
Number 95. Station Road, I.
It was the last house in a row of 14 substantially built brick dwellings.
Pauline, the only child for 11 years now has a brother John.
About this time Pauline left the junior village school for Ibstock community college.
These were very unhappy times for Pauline, she was labelled as a dunce and an uncooperative pupil. This brought her many punishments.
Nowadays she would have had special tuition as being severely dyslexic.

Friday night was 'bath night,' at Pauline's, and many other homes too.
The water was heated in a large cast-iron copper, with a coal fire burning underneath.
A large six-foot tin bath was filled with hot water, Pauline went in first, then her mother followed by dad who was a coal miner.

Although the water was never completely changed, a bucket full was taken out and topped up with hot water from the boiler for the next one.

Granny Finney's front room was a sweet shop, this was Pauline's first stop after returning from school, Granny always gave her sweets.

Pauline is still a sweetie to this day and surprisingly has only two teeth missing through an abscess.

Uncle Jim stayed with them for many years and loved to play tricks on Pauline. The most memorable one was one Christmas, Jim placed the coal in Pauline's stocking, Pauline retaliated by filling uncle Jim's shoes with tomato sauce.

Unfortunately for Pauline's uncle, Jim had the last word by picking her up and dunking her in the water tub.

Hooray, the school has finished for Pauline. She is now 15 years of age, or has it?

Pauline started work as a cutter at the Wolseley hosiery factory in Leicester as a trainee cutter.

Leaving home at 7 am and not returning until 7pm. Later Pauline obtained a situation much nearer home as a loom weaver, a position she held until the birth of our first son Steven in 1954.

Pauline Centre
Pantomime chorus girl

Chapter 6
Teenage social life

Saturday night, was always dance night.
In almost every town and village hall a dance band playing the latest hits.
With my friend Vick and David, we decided to take lessons at a dance school in Shepshed.

First lesson, how to take a young lady in the hold.
I was a very shy young man and certain experiences can be unnerving.
However, in true British grit, I carried on to the end of the course making many friends.
Pauline and her friends also went dancing however, since she was three years my junior she would not have left school at this time.

I played for Grace Dieu cricket club for many years with some great lifelong friends, traveling many miles to away games on our bicycles.

When I was 18 years of age and old enough to go into the public house with my friend Vick Burton, we had a small beer and played darts.
We became quite good at this game of darts and very soon taking on all challenges.

Pauline tells a story of when she first went into town with friends after leaving school.
A certain establishment had a dubious reputation, nothing new in that.
However, someone reported to Pauline's father that she had been seen going inside.
Unfortunately for Pauline, her dad pounced upon her not waiting for an explanation.
It was not Pauline, but a young lady with the same color coat as Pauline wore.
Around that time Pauline's father bought her a Collard and Collard baby grand piano and paid for lessons.
A very expensive mistaken identity.
Things moved on much the same until I was 20 years of age and Pauline almost17.
Although I spent some of my free time on my uncle's farm, I was an apprentice plumber.
My first tutor was Claud Bradshaw a veteran of the first world war.
My first job every morning was to go around the village shops trying to obtain cigarettes.
During this time, just after WW2 tobacco was very scarce. Claude retired after a short time and was replaced by Harry Foster.
Harry was a joy to work with.

Unfortunately, the company ceased trading and I was temporarily unemployed.
I continued my apprenticeship with R. J. Shaw, Burton-on-the-Wolds, until I was called to do my National Service.

Chapter 7
Boy Meets Girl

I was with my mate Vick Burton, now long since passed away.

We were waiting in the Rex picture-house queue, in Coalville one Friday night early in 1950.

In front of us stood this young girl with her friend.

She had this magical sparkle in her eyes.

I was hooked at once although she was unaware of me.

Vick and I spotted her around the 'Monkey Walk', (that's where youngsters walked up and down the High street in Coalville), but she was always chatting to others. No change there then.

Dance venues were the rage at that time like the swimming baths in Coalville that were boarded over during the winter months and used as an entertainment venue.

The Rink at Swadlincote was very popular where we travelled to and fro by bicycle.

This particular Saturday, Vick Burton and I decided to go to the Holy Cross-school, Parson Wood hill Whitwick.

They had a first-class Assembly hall and still have today.

Dance bands played at all these venues; most popular were the bands that produced the Glen Miller sound.
Bands in those days meant musicians.
As we entered I spotted Pauline, our eyes met, and we smiled at each other, magic. She was dancing around with a friend, a girl I tried to separate her from, much like a sheepdog splitting a young female from the rest of the flock, well two's company and threes a crowd. It took some weeks for me to succeed.
Quickstep, Waltz and Foxtrot, were the most popular with the Jive making inroads, a legacy of the American forces that were stationed in this country.
I was quite an accomplished dancer having taken lessons for three years.
The rule with ballroom dancing is to hold the lady close, and I loved holding Pauline close and still do every day.
   Pauline had a brother some 10 years younger whilst I was the eldest of six. Taking Pauline home for the first time was quite scary for both of us, although my family was quite excited.
Pauline came from a (privileged) working-class background, she had her grand piano in the front room, where she played (in-between cuddles) the latest hits. I still

remember the words today, and the notes she taught me to play.

However, they didn't have what we had, a 9ins. Bush television.

She told her parents, "they have six children and a TV."

To visit Pauline's house in I was quite a long way from Whitwick.

I either had to travel on my bicycle or catch the Midland red bus.

I must admit that I missed several attendances at evening classes just to be with Pauline.

We did most of our courting around I, in an area that was (or maybe still is) generally known as the black Lane.

Picking the primroses on the banks of the railway was an activity we speak about to this very day, along with the occasional cuddle of course.

We became engaged to be married after a very short romance. Pauline selected the ring from the window of jewellers in Coalville, often checking to see if it was still there whilst I saved.

An engagement Photo

Chapter 8
Attention!

National service was from the age of 18, I was an apprentice so deferred until my 21st birthday.

Although I was excited at this new adventure, I had a dread of leaving Pauline.

There would be no more good night cuddles for six weeks.

I had a lovely letter from His Majesty King George VI asking me to join him at Budbrooke Barracks in Warwickshire on Thursday 20th September 1951, just eight days before my 21st birthday. He sent me a free train ticket and bus pass, and I was even going to be collected at the station; great!

You've guessed it, the King didn't turn up, just an army truck, driver and a sergeant with a red sash over his shoulder,

He ticked us off one by one on his notepad and then began the drive to Budbrooke barracks.

The first letter I wrote was to Pauline Ward, my 17-year-old girlfriend dated 21/9/1951, it was the shortest letter I have ever written to her.

It starts,

My dearest Pauline, today is Friday, at 1 o'clock, we were messed about last night until 11 pm drawing our kit. I shall not have time to write to Mother today, so give her my address and ask her to send my ration book asap. We are due to see the Dock later for jabs, etc.

Square bashing on Monday.

They gave me a HAIR CUT first day.

I am in the Royal Leicestershire Regiment.

All my very best love Jeff.

Not the most romantic letter ever written to a loved one, but I wasn't in a romantic mood. I noticed that I had spelled my name with a J, wonder when I became Geoff.

I will always remember the first few nights in Hut 6, 'A' company.

Twenty young men, between eighteen, and twenty-one years of age.

Bob was the only man I knew, he was also from Whitwick.

We made straw (paillasse) mattresses; they gave us two blankets and a pillow, but no sheets or pillowcases.

Grown men (unwilling conscripts) whimpering in the night wanting to go home to their lovers, or maybe mothers.

That was the Army way of creating a quick sharp shock; don't think recruits would stand for that today.

I recounted every aspect of my training in my letters to Pauline, as well as plenty of lovely stuff.

How some days the food was inedible and others it was quite enjoyable.

Looking back I think the food was always the same, the main problem I was missing both mine and Pauline's mum's cooking.

However I had been brought up on wartime rations in a household of eight with five siblings, nothing was ever refused.

After weeks of square bashing, PE and cross-country runs, we looked forward to every meal

Chapter 9
Our Wedding Day

Our wedding day was on Saturday 15th of December 1951, at the 'Church of the Holy Rood' Bagworth.

Uncle Alex was my best man as we sat in church waiting anxiously for my beloved to arrive on the arm of her father.

The wedding march burst forth from the organ, the long-awaited moment had arrived.

I stored it smartly to attention as if I was on parade.

I burst with love as I watch Pauline walking down the aisle on the arm of her father, and still do today.

She was attended by seven bridesmaids and two pageboys.

We made our marriage vows in the presence of God and a packed. very old Norman church,

The reception was held in the village hall, with some 140 guests attending a sumptious spread, all provided by Pauline's mum and friends.

There was a downside to that day, I had an abscess in my left armpit, causing me great pain throughout the day and night.

Not a night of married bliss we had hoped for as we cuddle together in bed at her parents' house.

I returned to barracks on Sunday evening, the medical officer put me on, 'excused all duties the following day.

I languished in pain in Hut 4, Budbrook Barracks when I should have been comforted at home with my young wife. Pauline also went back to work on Monday.

.

Chapter 10
Reunited with Pauline

I remember vividly stepping out onto the platform at Bagworth thinking 'home at last,' I shouldered my kitbag, and with my case (I still have it) containing all my presents, set off the quarter-mile walk to Pauline's home.

People hailed me in the street as I walked home, one lady told Pauline afterward that she broke down and cried as she witnessed my return.

Pauline lived in the end terrace of a coal-board house; it was number 95 Station Road Bagworth.

I spied through the keyhole in the back gate and Pauline was in the yard, I opened the gate and we met in each other's arms, it was strange at first, I will admit, but after a few kisses and cuddles (we still have these every day) everything was back to normal.

Paulina accompanied me the next day as I returned my kit and got my discharge from Ripon barracks.

The only thing I regretted leaving there was my army greatcoat, we had so many cuddles in it when on leave from Budbrooke barracks.

I changed into my civvies, and we caught the bus to Ripon station and the train to Derby.

Too late the last train for home had gone, so we spent the night cuddled up on Derby station until the first train next day.

I had been parted from Pauline for almost 20 months of our newly married life. During that period, I had insisted that she led a normal life socialising with her friends. Our life has always been based on love and trust.

We lived with Pauline's mother and father for the first few months until we obtained a small rented cottage in the village of Whitwick.

Id managed to octane a job with C V Lane and son plumbing and heating engineers in Coalville.

Work started at 7:30 am till 5 pm with a 30-minute break for lunch. My only transport was my trusty bicycle, so to cover the 4.8 miles it was 6:30 am depart from home.

Pauline also worked in Coalville, catching the Midland red bus at 7:30 am. She was a weaving loom operator.

Chapter 11
On Silver Street.

My mother had managed to obtain this very small cottage standing in the back yard of number 2, Silver Street Whitwick. The cottage backed onto the school playground where I played as a boy a few years earlier.

We certainly had some fun and great adventures fending for ourselves for the first time.

Pauline soon became pregnant much to the delight of our family, their first grandchild.

We had a small living kitchen with a coal-fired cooking range. Alongside was a white kitchen sink with cold water tap over.

We often look back at the time when Pauline put the chicken into the oven with all the giblets inside encased in a plastic bag.

The egg custard she served that wasn't cooked.

It was a very steep learning curve but we made it in the end.

We had many an enjoyable evening listening to the radio, it was quite expensive at the time however we still have the same radio today and it is still in good working order on one longwave station.

Our small bedroom had an open coal fire, cold nights became snugly.

Coal was very expensive and I relied on dad for some of his monthly allowance from the coal mine where he worked. That I had to fetch in a wheelbarrow the distance of the round-trip 1 mile.

On other occasions, I scavenged the spoil bank of our local colliery gathering what small pieces of coal I could find.

This was extremely dangerous and illegal but needs mus.

I had a small allotment next to dads where I managed to grow plenty of vegetables, life was hard but we were happy.

At the end of June 1945 for our first baby was due to be born.

We agreed to stay at Pauline's mums during this time as it was going to be a home birth.

Steven Paul arrived two weeks later with the help of the local midwife.

It was a difficult birth and took Pauline some time to recover before we managed to move back home.

I believe that Pauline was 11 years old when brother John was born so she did have some baby caring experience.

Steven had quite a few medical problems as a baby, asthma, and eczema racked his body.

Pauline accompanied him on many long bus journeys to the hospital for treatment over many years.

The only transport we had was a bicycle. That was normal for most people so we didn't feel left out.

I was a journeyman plumber, that's a fancy name for riding your bicycle between different properties to make repairs or re-washer taps et cetera.

One day I rode past a small new housing development and came across an old workmate.

There were just six semi-detached houses with bathroom and hot water system.

Unfortunately, they were all sold, but he did know where there was one for sale in the next village.

Within a few months, we had moved into a new house. number 84 Parson Wood Hill.

Chapter 12
84 Parson Wood Hill

It seems strangely unreal looking back at the documents regarding the purchase of our new house.

The purchase price was £1625, our deposit was £100 with a monthly mortgage repayment of £8.4s 6p over a 25year period.

I worked 5 ½ days per week and brought home 10.10 shillings.

Our semi-detached house was basic without central heating, or roof insulation, or even cooking facilities.

I signed a hire purchase agreement at the local hardware store for a new gas cooker. We were now able to move in.

Our biggest expense was to hire a specialist removal company for Pauline's grand piano.

If I remember correctly they charged me £12, representing over one month's mortgage repayment, but as you know #ilovethatgirl

Many of the housing developments in the UK give little space between properties.

Fortunately, our new neighbours where Winnie and Stan Blakemore, they had an 11-year-old son William.

They were almost 15 years our senior and always ready to help, however helping out in childbirth never occurred to Winnie in her wildest dreams.
Julie our daughter was expected 18 months after we had moved in.
Unexpectedly Pauline went into labour, I asked Winnie if she would stay with Pauline whilst I dashed om my bicycle to fetched the midwife.

Unfortunately for Winnie, our daughter decided to make an early appearance.
Fortunately, the midwife was at home and when I told her of the urgency she left in her car at once.

You have a daughter, the midwife shouted down the stairs as I arrived home a few minutes later.
That story got re-counted many times and may even have been embellished slightly.

Chapter 13
Late 1950's

I write this paragraph in August 2020. just as our great-grandchildren start the new academic year, their ages ranging from 5 to 16 years of age, reminding us when our young family started infant school.

A new village school had recently been built only a few hundred yards away from our house.

Steven was now ready for his first day. He stayed without much trouble until it came mid-morning, running in-home declaring, "I've had enough."

However, Miss Swain the headteacher was close behind.

No one ever got the better of Miss Swain and Steven returned with her in silence.

During this time Pauline enrolled for an evening class, dressmaking was her preference, whilst I looked after the children.

Not only did Pauline make dresses for herself but also clothes for the children. She even made me a two-piece suit that I wore with pride.

Having younger children allowed Pauline to make new friends, and some remain to this day.

Going on holiday had never really occurred to us as a possibility until Stan, our neighbour suggested we book a caravan at Ingoldmells, a popular seaside resort on the east coast of England.

He agreed to take us down and collect us at the end of the holiday completely free of any charge.

The paid holiday at that time was just the first week of August.

This was not the large spacious holiday caravan we see on site today, but more like a touring caravan.

We had to take our bed linen and towels everything else was provided.

Fortunately, Stan knew exactly where we were going having holidayed here previously.

The children were very excited as we made up the beds for the evening.

We decided on a fish and chip supper having
noticed a chippy as we approached our destination.

After an hour Pauline had not returned and I was desperate, not daring to leave the children alone, all kinds of possibilities running through my mind.

There was a gentle knock on the door, Pauline had completely lost her bearings amongst the multitude of caravans.
The next morning the chippy was visible from our caravan, we laugh at this event many times.

Chapter 16
Swinging sixties

The 60s were an eventful time locally with the building of the M1 motorway through our area and the new Belvoir shopping precinct in Coalville.

I also passed my driving test in dad's car, however buying a motor vehicle was financially out of the question.

Pauline walked into town on Friday market day to do the shopping with the children in tow when not at school.

I had managed to get a better-paid job and things were looking good, when suddenly I was hospitalised with an abscess that was situated in a very delicate place.

Two weeks in Loughborough General Hospital and one week in Helen Towles convalescent home, with instructions on discharge not to return to work for a further week.

The financial situation was desperate so I returned to work immediately. The sale of Pauline's Grande piano helped us through this crisis.

During this period Commonwealth countries were looking for skilled workers in the construction industry.

A friend had already settled in Wellington
New Zealand and we had a desire to
follow.
We decided it was time to take this idea of
emigrating to Pauline's parents.
We caught the Midland red bus to
Bagworth via Coalville.
George, Pauline's dad, was in bed after his
Sunday pint at the working men's club
followed by is Sunday roast, a lifelong
tradition.
Teatime arrived table set for high tea, Julie
went upstairs to wake her grandad. "I can't
wake up grandad and he's cold," Julie said.
I think we all knew immediately that George
had died in his sleep.
The thought of emigrating to New Zealand
never entered our heads again.

That same year we had a proper holiday
in a private hotel,
along with our friends Alma and Des
Hemsley and their two boys.
It was memorable in lots of ways. Steven
managed to get his feet sunburnt `and
needed piggybacks most of the time.
Another time whilst having drinks one
evening, the young off duty waitress
walked into the bar.
Des shot out of his seat to buy her a drink.

On his returning Alma gave him a hefty kick under the table saying, "you know what that's for."
We never failed to remember that moment when in their company.
The following year both our families went to Boscombe in a private hotel. full board £27:6s

Quite a few important, and longlisting changes came about in1963.
I joined a small building company A H Wilson situated in the village of Ibstock, employing 17 people with the boss's son David in charge.
I was given a Morris Minor van and was able to use it privately.
No more cycling miles to and from work, Brilliant!
The Polio vaccine was given on a lump of sugar for the first time, unfortunately too late for my younger brother Fred, he had caught the disease earlier and one leg was permanently in a calliper.
President John F Kennedy was assassinated, the Profumo affair, and the famous Martin Luther King's speech, "I have a dream."
Pauline secured an evening job as a cleaner at our local clothing factory giving

her financial independence that I believe is very important.

This reminds me of our wedding day when I said to Pauline, "how much money do you have?"

"Half a crown," she said.

I never asked again although today 69 years on I do her online banking.

Our youngest son James came along in 1965.

Another home birth that was less traumatic than Julies.

The company expanded quite quickly and I was placed in charge of plumbing and heating department.

In 1968 the company opened a sales office in the Coalville precinct.

There was great excitement around the town as we had managed to engage Penny Plummer from New Zealand the newly crowned Miss world

to perform the opening ceremony.

Apart from the odd game of football I predominantly played cricket for Grace Dieu Park Cricket club.
Pauline would come along to the home matches and make the sandwiches and drinks for the interval.
Company commitments 5 ½ days each week soon put a stop to my playing days, although I attended match days whenever possible, and still do to this day.

The company had a private box at the Leicester City football club, occasionally I was invited to attend and take a guest with me.
A grand affair with food and drinks provided throughout the afternoon.
Because of the company's continued good fortune, the management was occasionally, taken to see the latest West End shows.

Chapter 17
Good morning campers

How it came about I am unable to remember, however, we borrowed an old scout tent and equipment and set off to the Lake district one Whitson bank holiday. After many trials and tribulations and help from experienced campers, it was finally erected and turned out to be a ridge tent with a bell end that contained two sleeping compartments.

Pauline and Julie in one with the two boys in the other, leaving yours truly to sleep in the main area.

Darkness fell and we were still chatting and laughing about our situation.

I was covered up with a plastic sheet to keep dryt as the rain started to fall.

"Speak as if you're in a reference library or you will have two leave the site." bellowed the warden.

He scared us and we went to sleep like naughty children.

Even to this day, we use that phrase if someone is shouting or talking loudly.

The next year, we purchased our frame tent and toured Scotland via the Great Glen.

Although we went camping at least once every year I would just like to recall these two incidents.

Our friends, Alma and Des suggested that we go on a camping holiday in France. What a great idea!

Our first-time ferry crossing went without a problem and we congratulated ourselves for meeting all the time slots allocated.

I never found it a problem driving on the right-hand side of the road or negotiating traffic islands although in a later story you may doubt that statement.

Desmond, our dear friend (now long departed) took several days before he would lead the way insisting on keeping to the left as in the UK.

After a two-week tour of Brittany and Normandy, we returned to our last camping site near the ferry port of Caen.

Alma was not a happy bunny; the washing and shower facility was communal.

She was a very private person.

It was the first campsite we had come across that supported a takeaway selling frog's legs and snails.

We didn't try them but our younger son James did and thought the frog's legs tasted like chicken.

Our last ever venture was to Brothers Water in the Lake District.
A fantastic area with walks around the lake and into the hills.
Everything was perfect, well at least for the first few days.
During the night the heavens opened and we were awakened by the sound of tents being dismantled.
We lay a while snuggled in a warm bed until Pauline decided to take a peep out.
"Think you should take a look outside, "said Pauline.
The whole of the site was underwater.
We managed a quick cup of tea and a slice of toast threw everything into the boot and headed home over the Pennine Way.
We loved that tent and kept it many years, the grandchildren love to play in.
Time to buy a caravan!

Chapter 18
Looking Back

It's September 28, 1975, and we are moving to a new detached home, a short distance away from Parson Wood Hill.
We thought it would be a good time to look back at our achievements and failures during those 18 years.

Steven, our eldest son was an apprentice electrician.
Julie, our daughter had just started work at our local chemist whilst James our youngest son attended Castle Rock school.
We made many improvements to that house over the years, although when I look back we must have been the neighbours from hell with all the alterations I did, "sorry girls if you read this. "

I knocked two rooms into one, extended the kitchen, built a stone fireplace, and move the heating boiler to an external position, not forgetting the bar with a glass top and tile roof.
I kept bantams at the top of the garden, not a problem to anyone providing they didn't mind the cockerel growing in the early morning.

I am unable to remember why I built a dovecote and kept four white doves.
Seemed a good idea at the time I suppose. Unfortunately, it didn't turn out that way as they seemed to prefer the veggies on my neighbour's garden to the corn I fed them on.

On the bright side, I was made a director of the company I worked for and now had a company car. No more placing a plank across the wheel arches of the van for our family to sit on.
All this before seat belts were introduced

Pauline also managed to pass her driving test we all thought she was brilliant, which of course she was.

About this time my grandmother Agnes Walker passed away in her 83rd year.
She had retired from farming life to live in a small brick-built cottage with roses growing round the front door, a typical English cottage in Gelesmore.
I have passed it many times over the last 45 years and it is still the same today.

We were sad to leave our friends and neighbours after 18 years of memories, sad to leave our garden with grandma Walkers gift of a pear tree too established to move.

Chapter 19
Swallow Dale

Saturday, the 28th of September 1974, we were on the move to Swallow Dale. A four-bedroom detached house with dining room and garage situated on the edge of Charnwood forest.

The price was £10,000 and as I write this 45 years later a similar property nearby just sold for £300,000.

Although we missed the old house, the extra space was welcome especially with Stephen and Julie now at work and James at secondary school.

This was a large development with Grace Dueu brook running through the site.

We were the first people to occupy one of the new homes and wondered who our neighbours would be.

It turned out to be Richard and Janet Prasinski with young daughter Anna. Wonderful people, although they only stayed a few years we are still in contact with them to this day.

Other families have since come and gone and it has always been a sad day when they departed.

Twenty-four properties were built on our side of the bridge and occupied first.

Most households had younger children of school age so socialising with one another was quite easy and this led to many activities which carried on in tradition for many years. I recall a one-off activity that took place between the families on our side of the brook against those from the other, a tug of war challenge.

The object was simple, which side entered the brook first.

They thought it was too strenuous for me (at 44 years of age) to take part so I was given the task of captain. After bellowing out to manage to keep the team in time I finally lost my voice.

I am not sure which team won or if anyone did it was a great social occasion, wound up with a few beers and jacket potatoes.

Guy Fawkes night was another celebration with fireworks held on the flood plain a short distance away.

Then supper with every household contributing, Pauline was famous (and is so today) for making traditional bonfire toffee.
Great times we shared with many wonderful people

A faded photo, but you get the idea.
Helen, on the piano now lives in Spain, the girl with the brolly is our granddaughter Samantha.
Between the pair is Chris Emmett.

Chapter 20
Treading the Boards.

We are fortunate that in the village we have a very healthy and active community spirit with meetings at, 'The Charles Booth Centre.'
Pauline along with Chris Reddington joined Thringstone pantomime society within a short time of moving to the area, today it is known TPADS www.tpads.org.uk
Pauline and Chris were just two of the troop of the dancing girls.
She performed it for four- or five-years giving way to younger girls.

About the same time Roy Ramsel, an accountant from work introduced me to Moira male voice choir.
I was new to choral singing and I was positioned in the first tenor section of the choir.

We toured the local area extensively and took part in many national choral competitions obtaining several firsts.
The choir was asked to sing at several royal occasions including singing to Princess Diana.
An invitation to sing at the Royal Albert Hall with the massed choirs was another special occasion,

Every year the choir did a charity tour in some part of the UK, staying at a local hotel where we always had an evening's DIY entertainment.
Sadly, the choir has now ceased to exist owing to younger people no longer interested in that type of singing.
I was its last president.
However, I can't leave you without telling of the time we toured France and it involves Pauline.
The Saturday evening concert was in the town of Montage.
I can't pretend we had a huge audience but it was acceptable.
Afterwards, we were all transported to a local hotel for a champagne reception.
The hour was late, and the champagne was chilled and sparkling.
Not the best combination for some people especially Pauline.
She swears to this day that she only had one glass however the results were devastating.
Upon meeting the cool night air Pauline sparked out and had to be carried both on and off the coach.
I had to undress her and put her to bed, her reputation damaged forever, in a nice way of course.

David Garner greeted Pauline many times over the years with, "remember Montage Pauline."

Moira male voice choir giving a Sunday concert at Arnesby Methodist church I am in the back row 1st left

After the choir I was asked to join TPADS in one of their musicals, I must admit it did come as a shock as I had no acting experience.

I am grateful to Mandy Baghurst for giving me that chance.

 Nowadays I can be found singing in the Coalville community choir.

Sing loud be proud.

Chapter 21
Crafty Pauline

One date I will remember is the 4th of May 1979 when Margaret Thatcher was elected Prime Minister of the UK and Northern Ireland.

I was extending our single garage into a double to accommodate Pauline's first car, a Vauxhall Victor automatic.

She was now able to visit her elderly mother in Bagworth more frequently without the tedious bus journey, also taking up part-time employment in many different situations over the coming years This continued for many years until funding cutbacks were made by the Leicestershire county council around 2008.

I just need to skip back a few years to record a momentous event in Pauline's life. In her 69th year, she decided to apply and was accepted into the sixth form of King Edward the seventh college as an A level student in art and design.

You may remember me telling you previously that Pauline was severely dyslexic.

I was very worried about her relationship with the other students. How would they react to her disability?

Times had changed for the better and Pauline was welcomed with open arms by other students.

We waited in trepidation the next few months until the results letter dropped through the door.

It was a C pass.

She threw the letter up into the air in disgust at only getting a C, until one of our grandchildren told her it was better than they had done.

The years of torment she suffered at school were put to bed at last.

Chapter 22
Marathon runner.

"Join us for the first Coalville marathon," were the headlines of the sports page in our local newspaper.

This was 1981 and I'm now 51 years of age and thinking it would be a great idea to enter. Entrance fee paid, now how does one go about training for a marathon?

I bought my running gear from a local outlet and started doing short jogs.

My body threw a whoopsie and complained bitterly.

I did some research and discovered, 'Fartlek training.' or interval running.

This suited me fine, as soon as I became fatigued I just walked, perfect!

I now had basic fitness with approximately six months to build up to marathon capability.

Every weekday morning before I went to work I ran and walked a 3-mile circuit that was to be part of the marathon course. Saturday, I did a 5-mile run Sunday was my rest day.

Although my morning training remained the same, I did build up my Saturday run to about 13 miles.

Marathon day finally came with great excitement around the village.
Many local young men and ladies taking part.
I wasn't last but not far off, finishing with a large blister on my left foot I hobbled into the ambulance treatment tent to loud applause from Pauline and family.

Next was Paris, a memorable run, especially when passing through the Arc de Triomphe.
Athens, the original Marathon as part of a holiday with Pauline combined with the, Physically Handicapped and Abled Bodied charity.
Although every handicapped person had a personal carer on a proposed trip to the Acropolis at least two helpers were required if it was to go ahead so all the marathon party agreed to help.
It was a most memorable and satisfying experience even made the Greek TV evening news.

Race day. A bus journey to the starting point in Marathon then a 42.195km uphill run to the old Olympic stadium in Athens to be greeted by Pauline cheering from the stone terraces.
An experience I will never forget.

I managed to gain entry to the London Marathon as an independent runner.

I caught the National Express bus from Coalville direct to London on the day before the race.

The starting point for the seniors was different from the mass start and was overjoyed when I knew that I was on the correct underground train.

It was a beautiful sunny morning not too hot and I set off on a very easy jog.

I didn't realise it at the time, but I lost a lot of energy interacting with the crowd giving high-fives. Next time, (what next time?) I will keep to the middle of the pack.

Yours Truly on the 2nd lap of the
1st Coalville Marathon.
Chapter 23
Bonne journée

In the late 1980s daughter Julie and husband Andrew with their two young children Jane and Carl thought it would be a good idea to sell their off-license store in Shepshed and move to France.

A few years earlier company management closed my mechanical services department in favour of independent contractors.

I was offered another position but decided to take redundancy and start my own business, 'Fitted Kitchens & Bathrooms.'

I am mentioning this because I had just completely refurbished their bathroom.

We were devastated by the news of our grandchildren moving to France.

They eventually purchased an old farmhouse with outbuildings on a large plot of land.

La Vourie, Mount Jean, Sarth. Normandy France.

Outstanding features of the property were, outside earth toilet and a cold water tap in the garden.

A charming feature (as the estate agents say) comes with complimentary bats in the attic.

July holiday fortnight came around and we set off with our touring caravan to board the overnight ferry from Portsmouth to Carn.

We had an overnight cabin with breakfast served.
Make the most of every moment is my motto.
Down to the car deck and away, well not quite.
I must have left the side lights on; the battery was flat.
This is not unusual, as a starter truck quickly appeared and we were away.
As I mentioned in a previous chapter I have no problem with driving on the right and side of the road.
Okay Pauline I may have gone down a one-way street in the opposite direction, but it was early morning, and nothing was about.
 We eventually arrived safely.
Carl and Jane quickly made their beds in our caravan bunks, so escaping the bats in the attic for the next two weeks.

.

    We made the same journey the following year. This time they had installed a bathroom and a flush toilet as well as electrical power.
Our daughter Julie had secured a position at the village school with preschool infants.

It was an open day at our grandchildren's school which was situated in the nearby town.
The headmaster told me he could not distinguish between our grandchildren and local children in a conversation.
Made us very proud.

The next day along with our daughter and grandchildren we set off with the caravan to explore.
About 20km later disaster struck, we were hit broadside on a crossroads completely writing off our car.
Fortunately, the caravan held us in check and I only had minor injuries, and the others just shaken.
A local family invited us into their home for a coffee whilst the police were called; we were breathalysed and accident claim forms were completed.
The local garage stored our car until arrangements could be made for collection
He then transported us along with our caravan back to Mont St. Jean.
The family who was so kind to us said, "there is an accident on these crossroads every week. "
Green flag breakdown service collected us on the day and time for our boat return crossing after collecting the car from the garage. a brilliant service.

The next year we caught a plane from our local airport to Paris then the TGV to Le Mans where our family was waiting to collect us.

The next year they sold the property and returned to England.

Our granddaughter Jane is now head of languages at a college in Leicester.

Carl has followed me into the construction industry as a surveyor.

Our annual fortnightly caravan holidays continued in the UK with our three other grandchildren, Emma, Kylie, and Samantha until they were too old to come with us.

We did travel abroad on holidays on our own that I will recount later.

Chapter 24
Life's challenges

Our journey through life has brought many hardships, as well as bestowing many blessings upon us.

In the last 40 years, Pauline has spent some period of every year in the hospital.

We were having a lovely time in Tenerife when during the night I had to call the emergency doctor to attend Pauline.

He took one look at her and after I had paid him his callout fee transported us to the hospital which fortunately was only two blocks away.

She was placed under observation for five days.

Diagnosis, constriction of the bowel.

Unfortunately, our insurance company would not pay as this had happened once before, which made it an expensive holiday.

However, we did enjoy the last seven days together.

This has happened a further 20 times since that occasion but only twice whilst on holidays in the UK.

I will just mention one other time when Pauline was in the Queens medical unit Nottingham for five weeks.

She became so friendly with the staff we were invited to a nurse's wedding.

As I write this she is just recovering from being chased by a spider, resulting in a nasty accident.

Four weeks in the hospital, four weeks recovering at home.

Pauline is always cheerful, well mostly.

As for me! Lymphoma at the age of 63 put an end to my business although I worked through the first three months of my treatment to complete my obligations. Just a couple of other nasties so we can get onto the good stuff.

After a non-stop downpour of rain lasting six hours the beautiful Grace Dieu brook that so many of you have admired on Instagram and Facebook flooded our house.

Alterations downstream have since been carried out.

I am in the process of installing flood barriers to the doors, you never know with global warming.

Another incident whilst out at the end of term college musical, on returning home our house had been ransacked by thieves, more devastating than the flood.

They took all of Pauline's jewellery, her mothers, and her grandmothers.

Worst of all her engagement ring that took me so long to save for, Pauline checking the jewellers window weekly to make sure someone else hadn't purchased it.

They were disappointed regarding cash as we are never kept any in the house we had just a few euros left from our previous holiday in France.

Although I was the eldest of six children by seven years I have already lost two brothers and a sister.

Pauline has a younger brother by 11 years who is doing okay.

Now for our blessings.

Our family, we were blessed with two boys and a girl, five grandchildren, and 10 great-grandchildren.

Our youngest granddaughter Samantha was due to be married in November 2020 however the Corina virus infection put it back to February 2021. Not sure if we will make it in person but no doubt we will be able to witness it via the Internet.

Just a few of our great grandchildren
During an interval in the Sound of music
with grandpa Walker

Chapter25
After lymphoma

It took me two years to recover from this devastating illness and get a reasonable amount of strength back.
By this time, I was 65 years of age and able to take my pension.
Pauline was busy with her crafts, visiting craft fairs, and even taking some private classes.
I helped whenever I could with setting up displays in our caravan awning.
However, I had worked without a day's unemployment from when I was a boy and now finding it difficult being at a loose end.
I started running again and entered a few local 5 and 15K events, some with our grandchildren, but that was recreation.
Many years previous I had shown an interest in making a large rocking horse and Pauline had bought me a plan.
I purchased a very old but reliable lathe from eBay to make the stand also wood carving tools to shape the horse.
I was able to buy the roughly shaped pieces from the Rocking horse shop.
It certainly kept me busy for the next three months, carving the head was the most difficult.

It was a dapple-grey rocker and although you can buy transfers for a professional paint job, I finished it all by hand.
I continued woodturning for several years until my failing eyesight made it too dangerous for me to continue.

Snowy stands in our dining room waiting for our great-grandchildren to ride.

Although Pauline is proficient in many types of crafts I like her carved and decorated eggs the best.

It's fascinating to watch her cut intricate shapes in an Ostrich or Emu egg with a mini disc cutter.

At the time of writing this Pauline is concentrating on knitting.

There is one thing I will never understand about Pauline, and I am sure she will not mind me mentioning it.

She avoids technology at all costs mobile phones especially yet she can program her computer sewing machine. #ilovethatgirl

Chapter 26
Life's Challenges

Every year Pauline would help to organise a trip to the National Exhibition Centre in Birmingham where crafters and companies for a two-week period displayed and sold their work.

I always enjoyed going along, they had woodwork stalls that were of interest.

I always wandered off on my own making arrangements to be at the assembly point for the journey back home.

I suddenly felt very hot and sweaty and slowly walked out for some fresh air.

I set out to find Pauline, an almost impossible task in such a vast complex. Fortunately, I spotted her making a purchase, she took one look at me and knew there was something wrong.

We walk slowly to the medical centre, they didn't like my blue appearance and called the ambulance.

The medical staff agreed to send a member to our coach departure point with the relevant information.

We arrived at the Queen Elizabeth Hospital quickly assessed and admitted. The problem now being that Pauline was 40 miles from home with no way of returning.

My mobile telephone with all our family telephone numbers was at home.
They decided to find Pauline accommodation for the night whilst they contacted family members from the addresses Pauline gave them.
Our son collected her the next morning.
After an angiogram the next day I was diagnosed with calcium restriction in an artery, an operation they were unable to perform so I was transferred across the city to Heartlands hospital where the procedure was successfully carried out.

Whilst getting back to full strength I decided to write some Christian poetry and songs aimed at young people.
Modern Bible poems Part 1 and Part 2
The printed booklets quickly sold with the proceeds to charity.
They can now be found on Amazon kindle.
The Ben's Adventure books started as a project between my brother Fred (a well know local artist) and myself as a way of raising money for local charities.
As with this book Instagram and Facebook friends come to my rescue with illustrations and content advice.
Then came "Parted by Conflict." ` story of my time as a National service soldier researched from hundreds of love letters

Pauline and I had exchanged over a two-year period.

They had been languishing in the attics for 60 years.

One thing I had been hoping to accomplish was the, "Hadrian's wall challenge. "a 23-mile event over torturous terrain, an event organised by the Alzheimer's charity.

Our grandson Carl came to visit one day and I mentioned to him that I would like to enter this event, "I'll take you Grandad," Carl said.

George my grandson in law also agreed to come along.

I had three months to train this time with walking boots on, haversack with food and water plus weatherproof clothing.

Our fortnightly caravan holiday was taken near some challenging walking trails.

Not for Pauline she had her knitting and I trained very early and Pauline was always supportive.

The challenge day soon came around and we booked a room nearby the Assembly point (and finishing post) which was at 6 am the next morning.

A convoy of coaches transported as to the starting point 20 miles away.

Not the best feeling when you know you must walk back over some of the most challenging terrain in the UK.

George and grandson Carl

Chapter 27
Time marches on

Looking back over the last 90 years, all from memory, Pauline and I have had many discussions and remarkably few disagreements.

We have always enjoyed raising money for charity in whatever way we could.

Pauline with her annual Christmas craft sale held at home and I mostly from sports events and book sales.

In 2015 The old schoolhouse a residential home for young adults with learning and physical disabilities.

They were looking for quite a lot of money to complete a light sensory room to stimulate certain of the young adults.

- **The Old School House**
- Learning Disability
- Physical Disability
- Sensory Impairment
- Younger Adults

We contacted all the groups that met in the village community centre and local churches and they made very generous donations.

The staff at the home went far beyond the call of duty raising thousands of pounds.
I had in a previous year put on a talent show in our local church as a fundraiser. This was quite successful so I decided to revive this and hold it in the village community centre.
Thringstone's Got Talent was the show. Nigel, Sound, and light, Shannon, hostess, Martin, stage manager.
Family and friends helping out on the night of the event.
I was to provide a minimum of 14 acts,
   The show was a roaring success in every way, the staff from the home brought the house down with their song and dance act.
   The show has gone ahead every year since always fundraising for a different charity until lockdown 2020.
   The government 2nd Corona 19 virus lockdown November 2020 is depriving many of their desire to visit family and friends.
Pauline and I haven't seen any of our great-grandchildren for almost 12 months, we will become strangers to them and the only fleeting glimpses of some grandchildren.

Chapter 28
Changes in our lifetime

The area in Leicestershire where Pauline and I grew up was scattered with deep coalmines, brickyards, hosiery, boot and shoe and loom weaving factories.
The surrounding Countryside farms had dairy herds.
Today all the coal mines have closed.
One brickyard remains and one small weaving factory.
I searched online for a boot and shoe factory, looks like the last one is student accommodation.
The monks at Mount Saint Bernard Abbey were the last farmers to sell off their dairy herds.
They have now set up a brewery, apparently, it is highly successful.
Water carried from the village pump or in my case a spring in the yard.
Earth toilets, a Friday night scrub in a tin bathtub.
Now many homes now have two bathrooms.
The old red telephone box on the village green with its 2 old pence to make a local call now a museum exhibit.
Every village had a police house where the village Bobby and his family lived.

Beware if you miss behaved.
A bicycle was the common form of transport for many getting to work.
Coal mining companies ran special busses.
I remember a street in our village that had oil lamps burning at night, later converted to gas, now they are all halogen.
Steam passenger trains ran frequently through most towns and villages, most are now long gone.
Communication by letter writing now taken over by email and texting.
Our family doctor would come and visit no matter what day or time you contacted him.
I could list many more.
 Some things remain unchanged like Ruby's fish and chip shop still serving the local community since 1895.
They stayed open through both World wars only coronavirus 19 has forced a temporary closure.

I think it was early 2014 when we joined Instagram, thought it would be a good idea for our extended family to see some of our daily activities.
All went well with an occasional video of Pauline doing her craft work and myself in the garden and short walk videos.
We had about 90 followers by the Easter Of 2015 when we suddenly noticed a few extra followers.
By the end of the week, I had 18,000' couldn't imagine why until I discovered that Lauren Skellett posted on Twitter, 'I know this old man who puts videos of his wife on Instagram. "I'm not quite sure what they expected to find, however, they couldn't have been too disappointed because most stayed and the following steadily increased until February 2020 when Pauline had her purse stolen while shopping in the town.
I appealed on Instagram and Facebook for the purse to be returned if found, we were not expecting bank cards or money but the purse was an old favourite of Pauline.
Never was it possible to imagine the reaction from social media.

Pauline had the offer of so many purses and wallets that we could have set up a

stall in the market. We thanked them for their kindness but didn't accept their offer.
 we had offers to appear on television and radio shows from many countries in the world.
We chose the good morning breakfast shows on both the BBC and ITV television also a spot on the local radio.
We now have a following of 350,000.
Best wishes Pauline and Geoffrey Walker
@geoffreywalk on Instagram.

Books also available on Amazon by Geoffrey Walker.
Ported by Conflict, paperback and Amazon kindle
Bens Adventures, paperback and Amazon kindle
Modern Bible poems 1 and 2 Amazon Kindle only.
You can read samples before you commit to buying I understand.

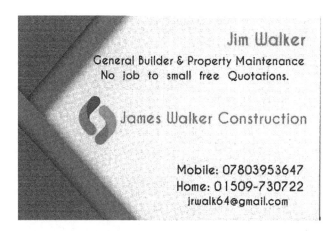
Louise Steel, local reporter for the Coalville Times and singer-songwriter who's just released a new album called 'Sideshow'.
Listen to her songs online
at: www.youtube.com/louisesteelmusicsite

Fish and Chip Shop LE67 8DD

Satisfaction Guaranteed

www.chums.co.uk

https://www.albionfarmshop.co.uk/about/

Rose of Stitching

http://www.roseofstitching.co.uk/
For that very special gift

Made in the USA
Las Vegas, NV
02 December 2020

11932195R00050